Docker

A Step-by-Step Guide to Learn and Master Docker

BRAYDEN SMITH

TABLE OF CONTENTS

Introduction

Innovation in today's fast-paced and interconnected society comes directly from the software. Developers need to be able to provide an intuitive, attractive, and easily accessible experience for their users in order to succeed. Docker's modern platform can provide that kind of innovation to all of its users with its unique method of packaging up applications into isolated, independent, and contained environments in order to maximize their portability as well as their efficiency. Docker has been referred to as "The modern platform for high-velocity innovation," and is currently the only independent container platform that can allow you to build, share, and even run any application easily and efficiently from anywhere you choose.

I would like to thank you for purchasing and downloading this copy of "Docker: A Step by Step Guide to Learn and Master Docker." I would also like to offer you a short word of congratulations for taking the first steps on the way to learning about, and mastering one of the world's most efficient and versatile platforms that can allow you to easily and seamlessly develop, ship, and run any application from anywhere you want. Of course, this refers to the Docker platform, which uses completely unique technology, referred to as the "container" to give Docker's users the ability to quickly and easily package up an application in a "contained" environment. These containers and the isolation that they provide can also allow for extra security in your application as well as the ability to run multiple containers at the same time without affecting performance.

Of course, there is a little bit more to the Docker platform than simply this "innovation." Docker is a unique platform for a tool that can be called nothing short of a "game-changer." Such a unique and innovative service like Docker and all of its various products and services will also inherently require a much higher amount of learning and adjustment in order to understand and master when compared to other similar services. There can be a bit of a "learning curve" with new and complicated services like this one, and approaching it can even seem a little bit intimidating at first.

This is why this book exists! This step by step guide to learning and mastering Docker is meant to help you do exactly what it says on the cover; learn and master Docker. This incredibly helpful book is meant to serve as your guide in understanding many of the various different products and services that Docker offers to its users, as well as a number of the different features that exist within those products and services and how to use them as effectively as possible in order to maximize the benefits of using this incredibly unique service. Additionally, this book will go over all of the little ins and outs of the Docker platform and its various products and services, including some tips, tricks, and shortcuts to help you even further in this goal.

This book will go over a number of different topics to give you all of the tools necessary to gain a complete understanding and mastery over Docker's various products and services. These topics include things like the various reasons why you would (and should) choose Docker over any other possibly similar service as well as some short introductions and guides to many of the various products and services that docker offers to its users such as Docker Enterprise and Docker Desktop for Mac or Windows, and the Docker Hub. This book will also go over many of the different features of Docker's various products and services, as well as how to actually use them at a fundamental level in order to help you to master this incredibly innovative platform for building and running applications as smoothly and efficiently as possible.

Chapter 1

Introduction to Docker

Docker can be a very useful tool for developers and system administrators, and can allow for much the much easier deployment of various applications by allowing its user to pack up those applications and their necessary resources into tidy and easy to access packages, which are referred to as "containers." Docker is described by Wikipedia as an open-source project that automates the deployment of software applications inside containers by providing an additional layer of abstraction and automation of OS-level virtualization on Linux. In simpler terms that will be easy to understand, this means that Docker is a tool that is meant to allow developers and system administrators to be able to deploy their applications within a discrete container that will allow that application to run much more easily and efficiently on a particular system. The primary benefit that docker is able to provide to its users is to box up (or contain) an application with all of the resources that it needs in order to function properly into one compact unit that is meant for software development. This is an incredibly innovative tool that is designed to help make it much easier for developers to build and run different applications on any system by using these containers. Containers can help in doing this by ensuring that an application will be able to run efficiently and easily by allowing developers to store their applications and all of their various part such as the libraries and other resources than the application needs in order to run properly into a container. By doing this, you will be able to make sure that all of your applications will be able to run the same way regardless of the system that they are being used on.

Docker is developed with the primary intention of being used for the Linux operating system. It uses a number of different useful features of the Linux kernel, such as kernel namespaces and cgroups, as well as a union compatible filing system that can allow for several independent containers to be run within a single instance of Linux. This can be very helpful in avoiding the overhead that can be experienced in starting up and maintaining a virtual machine. The support for namespaces within Linux can serve to isolate an application's scope of the operating environment. This includes things like mounted file systems, different networks, process trees, and user IDs. Additionally, the cgroups of the Linux kernel can provide resource limiting for the CPU and the memory of the system. As of version 0.9, Docker has also included a feature called the libcontainer library, which functions as docker's own methods of directly using various virtualization features that are provided by the Linux kernel, as well as using various abstracted interfaces designed for the purpose of virtualization. For these reasons, docker is used primarily by developers and system administrators and is designed with this in mind. For a developer, this means that you can focus solely on writing the code for your applications without needing to worry about its compatibility with a different system that it might be run on. It will also allow you to get a bit of a jump ahead by using one of several thousands of programs that are already designed to be run within a docker container as part of your own application. Docker can help to provide flexibility to developers and to system administrators in this way, and can greatly reduce the number of systems that are needed, due to its low overhead and smaller footprint.

Docker is, in some ways, similar to a virtual machine. However, it does also differ from virtual machines in that rather than trying to create an entire virtual operating system, docker will instead simply allow an application to use the same Linux kernel that the system it is being run on uses, and only requires that an application is shipped with the resources that it requires to run that are not already provided on the host system. This can allow the application to run much more efficiently and with a very significant boost to performance. It can also drastically reduce the application's overall size, too. Additionally, docker is completely open-source. This means that anyone can alter and contribute to docker in order to improve it or tailor it to meet their own specific needs if they require extra features that are not included by default. Docker is separated from virtual machines by its ability to utilize the resources that are already provided by the Linux kernel (especially with namespaces and cgroups) which can allow it to function without a separate operating system. Instead of a separate simulated operating system, like a virtual machine, a Docker container is able to build on to the kernel's functionality.

Containers can be somewhat difficult to understand, however. The basic idea of these containers was discussed briefly earlier in this chapter, but they should also probably be explained in more detail, as these containers will be the basis for most of the information to be contained in this book. A container can be described as a tight, discrete package that is designed to contain an application and all of the files that it needs to run in an efficient way that can allow them to stay isolated from the system that they are being run and hosted on. Containers have become more and more popular recently, as they can help to offer a much more logical packaging mechanism by allowing for specific applications to be run separately and independently from the system that they are being "hosted" by. This separation can allow container-based applications to maintain consistency easily and regardless of their current host system. This can include a wide variety of various environments, such as a public cloud, private data centers, or even the personal laptop computer of a developer of the application. This can give a developer the ability to build and test their applications in predictable, consistent environments that are isolated and controlled, which can allow for much more versatility, allowing the application to be run from anywhere.

Virtual machines have become the industry standard used to build and run software applications. Virtual machines run applications within another guest operating system, which is dependent on virtual simulation of the operating system, which is powered and maintained by the server's host operating system. A virtual machine can be very useful for providing complete isolation of various processes for applications in a number of different ways. For example, there are very few ways in which an issue in the host system's operating system is able to affect the software that is being run within the guest operating system and vice versa. However, this does come with a very high cost. There is also a very large amount of "overhead," which in this case refers to computational power that is effectively wasted and that is spent during the processes of starting up and maintaining the Virtual Machine, in order to simulate the host's hardware for a guest operating system.

Containers, on the other hand, have a slightly different method of approaching this task. A container can provide a large majority of the necessary isolation for these processes that a virtual machine can provide with much less overhead, using significantly lowered amounts of computing power than virtual machines, by using the much simpler mechanics of the host's operating system as opposed to virtually recreating the whole operating system.

Because of these unique benefits, containers (as well as docker, by extension) have been seeing widespread success. Large companies such as Facebook, Google, and Netflix have taken to using containers in order to help make large teams of engineers even more productive and to help in improving the efficiency at which those teams are able to utilize computational resources. Google has even credited the elimination of the need to possess and maintain large data centers to their adoption and use of containers.

Additionally, a lot of the technologies that power Docker's containers are completely open-source. This means that there is a large community made up of various contributors who all help to develop the products and a large number of similar or related projects that fit the needs of many different kinds of organization and groups. Arguably one of the most significant reasons for many people's recently sparked interest in this new container-based technology has been docker's "open source project" which is a command-line tool that has made creating and using containers much easier for developers as well as system administrators. Container technology has generated large amounts in interest in "microservice architecture," which is a specific method of designing and developing applications that involved breaking down more complex applications into several much smaller, more flexible portions that can easily work together. Each part of these applications is designed and developed independently, with the application as a whole being made up of all of these smaller pieces combined. Each of these pieces can be placed within a container and scaled separately from the rest of the larger, complete application.

Chapter 2

Why should you Choose Docker?

Based on the recent success of container technology, there are a number of reasons to utilize this incredibly useful and innovative tool. Docker has become the leader in the market of container technology by combining its container platform with a number of incredibly helpful services in order to help give developers all of the freedom that they require in order to effectively and efficiently build and maintain their applications without having to worry about becoming "locked-in" with a specific industry-standard technology. Many modern businesses have experienced a sense of pressure to transform their companies, but are limited by these kinds of applications and technologies that prevent them from doing so. Docker can help to remedy this issue by allowing these companies to "unlock their potential," giving them much more freedom and the means to develop their products with a container platform that can introduce their traditional applications and services to an automated, secure supply chain and allow them to improve collaboration within their companies.

Within modern companies, innovation is heavily reliant on powerful and effective software. Organizations that succeed in the modern marketplace are able to do so by becoming more software-oriented and by empowering their software developers to efficiently and effectively create new and engaging experiences for their customers. Naturally, these experiences will usually take the form of various applications that can run on a variety of different systems. Docker can allow a company to achieve all of these goals by giving them the best experience in developing useful applications that will allow for higher levels of success and cooperation within the company. In addition to allowing for much more ease in building useful and intuitive applications, the Docker platform also provides scaled security features that can continue to function without slowing the process of development. This is because of the fact that the docker platform has been built upon various industry-standard technologies with open source software such as Docker and Kubernetes. This platform is used by millions of individuals and companies around the world. Docker also includes a completely unrivaled library of content that is built for use with containers, which contains upward of 100,000 separate container images from various sources within the docker development community.

Docker has a number of incredibly useful and varied features. It can function efficiently with any programming, application framework, and even operating system. Docker can provide developers with the freedom to select the best tools for them and their uses, as well as various programming languages and appropriate application frameworks for any project that they might be working on. Docker Enterprise is one of the only container platforms that can give you

11

complete freedom of the operating system and infrastructure that you use. Docker can provide this type of excellence in a number of different areas. It has a number of useful features that can help developers to create applications that are efficient and easy to use while also streamlining the development processes for these applications. These features include various capabilities such as automated application scanning and signing for the purpose of policy enforcement, multi-layered security features, and the ability to build and deploy portable and secure hybrid cloud applications without getting in the way of the productivity of app development. There are a number of specific features that docker provides and various reasons why you should use Docker. These reasons will be detailed below:

Cost-effectiveness and returns on investments One significant advantage of choosing to use Docker is the return on investment. This is one of the most significant motivations behind a lot of management decisions, especially those regarding the selection of new products. The more a specific solution can reduce costs and overhead while also raising the profits of a company, the better this solution will prove to be. This applies especially to large companies that have already been established in their market and need to maintain a more long term source of steady revenue. In this way, docker can help to save developers money by drastically reducing their overhead in terms of both financial costs and infrastructure resources. Docker can allow for the need for much fewer resources of this type in order to develop and run various applications. Because of these reduced overhead costs, docker can allow businesses and other types of companies to save on

12

every aspect of their operations from the cost of maintaining servers to the employees that are actually needed in order to do so. Docker allows teams of engineers to be much smaller, and much more effective, enabling companies to maximize their efficiency and effectiveness.

Increased productivity. Docker containers can allow for higher levels of consistency in development and the standardization of the environment. This type of standardization is actually one of the most significant advantages of using a docker based architecture system. Docker can provide repeatable building, production, and testing environments as well. Being able to completely standardize the service infrastructures for all of the various parts of the operation can allow every member of a team to work more efficiently with each other and to communicate more easily with each other about various parts of the whole. By doing this, the team will be much more well equipped to efficiently find, analyze, and resolve any issues that exist in the application. This can help to increase efficiency and productivity for the team as well.

Container image efficiency. Docker can allow you to build a single container image and then use that image across all of the steps of the deployment process. This will allow you also to separate independent steps and to run them in parallel to each other. This can speed up the build to the production process by large amounts of time.

Compatibility. Docker allows you to eliminate the issue of compatibility for good. One of the largest and most significant benefits that docker can provide is "parity." With regards to docker, this means that all of your applications and images will be able to run the same way regardless of the device they are being used on. For a developer, this can make it much easier to actually develop their apps by spending much less time preparing environments for their applications. This will also make it much easier for you to maintain a stable production infrastructure at a basic level simply.

Simplicity! Another incredibly huge benefit that docker can provide is simplicity to its users. Users are able to use their own configuration without any issues. As docker is able to be used in a large number of environments, the infrastructure's requirements are no longer connected to the application's environment.

Quick and efficient deployment. Docker is a unique service in that it is able to reduce the time that it takes for deployment down to a matter of seconds. This incredibly fast deployment time is a result of Docker's unique container-based platform. Docker will create a container for each individual process that needs to be carried out, as opposed to booting an OS for those processes. This can also allow for quicker and easier creation and destruction of specific portions of information without having to worry about the processing power that is needed to bring it up again, becoming higher than can be allowed.

Continuous testing and deployment. Docker containers are configured by default to automatically maintain all of its dependencies and settings internally, in order to ensure environments that are as consistent as is possible at all stages of development. This allows Docker's users to be able to use the same containers while guaranteeing that there are no inconsistencies or unexpected variables during every step of development and production. However, if you ever need to make any sort of changes to a product during its release cycle, this can also be done quickly and easily. You can easily make any necessary changes to your containers and then test and implement any of those changes as well. The flexibility of Docker's containers is one of the most significant advantages of using this software, along with the other benefits that Docker can provide to its users.

Multi-cloud platforms. This is arguably one of the most significant reasons to choose docker over other options. Over time, there has been a very clear trend of major cloud computing service providers, such as amazon web services (AWS) and the Google Compute Platform (GCP) beginning to acknowledge and recognise the unrivaled availability and utility that Docker and its various services can provide to their users. Docker containers are able to be run inside of a wide variety of different platforms such as the Google Compute Engine, VirtualBox, and many others as well, as long as the host system's operating system is able to support Docker. Additionally, docker containers that are being run within one environment like an Amazon EC2 instance are able to quickly and easily be ported to other environments as well. Even if a container is ported to a new environment in this way, it will still maintain the same or similar consistency and functionality as the original environment, which can allow for a much smoother experience for developers and system administrators.

Isolation. Another very useful and attractive feature that docker can provide to its users is the isolation and segregation of all of your applications and resources. Docker ensures that every container has all of its own resources that are necessary for it to function and that those resources are completely isolated from those of other containers. You can even run multiple different containers for their own separate applications on completely separate stacks. Docker can help you by ensuring the clean and efficient removal of any application if this is necessary because all of your container-based applications are able to be run on their own separate containers. If you find that you do not need a particular application anymore, you can simply delete its container to remove it from your machine, and there will not be any files that are leftover from that application hiding within your host operating system. Additionally, docker can also make sure that each of its container-based applications is only allowed to use the resources that have already been assigned to those applications. Usually, a particularly "heavy" application might take up a lot of resources and cause a drop in the quality of performance or even downtime, but this is not a concern for container-based applications.

Security. The final benefit that will be listed here is another very important one. Again, docker can make sure that all of the applications that are running on containers are entirely separate and remain isolated from other applications and from the files on your host operating system. This allows Docker's users to maintain absolute control over the flow of traffic on the host, as well. A Docker container is never able to view any information about the files or processes that are running inside another container.

Chapter 3

Docker Products and Services

The Docker platform offers a number of separate integrated products and services that can be used to help you to build, run, and even share your container-based applications from your own system to the cloud. This is possible because the Docker platform has been based on the core building blocks of the docker brand and various tools that have come from Docker such as Docker Desktop, Docker Engine, and Docker Hub. Docker provides a number of incredibly useful tools that can help you to build, run, and share applications. Docker's desktop tools for developers can help you to streamline the process of delivering new container-based apps and tools and to make it easier and simpler to store applications that you have already build in containers moving forward. You will be able to run applications that are based on containers and manage those containers with services like the enterprise platform. You can even utilize tools like the docker container image library, docker hub, in order to accelerate your innovation. Docker hub can help you to explore millions of container images that have been made available by verified publishers within the community. As was stated previously, docker provides a large number of different services to help you in developing and distributing applications, which will all be described in more detail within this chapter.

Docker enterprise. This is one of Docker's biggest products. Docker Enterprise is the largest platform for applications that are based on container technology and allows you to build, share, and run all of your applications easily. Docker Enterprise can provide a secure supply chain for software and can deploy a wide range of applications to maximize its potential as well as your own. It can help in the automation of a number of tasks such as the provisioning of various containers, pods, and resources. Docker Enterprise also includes the docker universal control plane. This is Docker's own cluster management solution which can be installed onto your own system or in your private cloud and can help you to manage all of your applications and clusters from one place.

Docker Hub is another one of the incredibly useful tools that Docker provides to its users. Docker's Hub is a sort of common storage space meant to help developers share their own container files with others. The hub has a number of different developers and independent software creators that help to contribute content to it with their own container images from various open-source projects. Docker Hub's users can gain access to an unparalleled number of free public repositories of container images that other developers within the community have previously stored. With a paid subscription plan, Docker Hub's users can also gain access to its private repository feature, as well.

Docker also provides to its users a number of useful technologies. The first one to note is Docker's developer tools. These can help to improve developers to ship their applications much faster and make it much easier to build and run effective and useful container-based applications by extending the usefulness of the Docker Engine even further.

There is also a version of Docker that has been designed for Windows and macOS machines, called Docker Desktop. Docker Desktop is meant to run on the Windows 10 operating system, and cal allows windows users to do all of the things that Docker is designed to do for Linux users. This can allow developers to build applications for Linux as well as windows, and to share them easily. Docker Desktop is by far the easiest and most effective tool for building container applications for Swarm and Kubernetes with any framework or any language.

Docker also provides an open-source system for the automated management, routing, scaling, and placement of different containers, called Kubernetes. The Docker platform contains a secure kubernetes environment that is meant for developers of many different levels of skill. This can allow for the flexibility that is necessary for experienced users while also providing ease and convenience for newer users. The docker platform can also allow teams and individuals alike to run kubernetes interchangeably with swarm technology. This can provide a higher capacity for flexibility for users of the best tool for managing and using container-based applications.

Docker image registries can also allow you to securely store and manage your container images with your own personal registries. This is a feature that is included with the Docker Enterprise product and functions as a private image storage space for any container images that you wish to use it for. These registries can allow you to quickly and easily retrieve and build on to already existing container images. You can also create your own images yourself, as well, and then place them into your own repositories and share them with other individuals within your team or anyone else who you might wish to share them with. Security features that have been built in can also enable you and other people within your team to check on the source and the content within a container image, alongside a number of automatic functions and integration with CI/CD tools that can serve to speed up the testing and delivery of different applications.

Chapter 4

Docker Toolbox

This chapter will be about another incredibly useful feature that docker offers to its users, Docker Toolbox. The Docker Toolbox is by far the quickest way for you to get set up with Docker and begin developing your own applications. This toolbox can supply you with all of the various tools that you will need in order to get started with Docker. These tools include things like the Docker Client, Docker Machine, Docker Compose, Kitematic, and the Docker quickstart terminal app. Docker Toolbox is officially considered to be a legacy product and is meant for older Mac and Windows computers that do not meet all of the requirements for the current Mac and Windows desktop applications. If you are able to use the current Docker products, it is recommended that you do so. However, while docker Toolbox is a legacy product, Kitematic is still supported and is available for download as a separate product as well.

Docker Toolbox's various included products can cover a wide range of functions and will help you to get started as easy as possible. The Docker Machine and Virtualbox will allow you to run containers within a Linux virtual machine, which is maintained by the virtual box hypervisor. Kitematic is also a legacy product and comes bundled with the Docker toolbox. It is, of course, available to download on its own as well, however. Kitematic is an open-source solution that is meant to make the use of Docker on a Mac or a Windows PC much easier and more streamlined. Kitematic does this by automating the installation and setup process of Docker as well as providing an intuitive and simple graphical user interface to help you to run docker containers. It also works with Docker machine in order to supply a virtual machine and to install the docker engine to your system. The Kitematic user interface can supply you with various container images that you can then run right away. You are also able to use the search bar provided by Kitematic to search for specific container images that are available to the community. Or you can also use Kitematic's interface to help you to create and manage your container images quickly and easily. You can even switch back and forth between the Docker CLI and Kitematic's user interface if you want to do so. Kitematic can automate even advanced features such as volume configuration and port management.

In order to download and install Kitematic if you have not already, you can do so in a few ways. The first method of downloading and installing Kitematic is with Docker Toolbox. As was stated earlier in this chapter, kinematic is included with the Docker Toolbox application. Of course, Docker Toolbox is intended for older systems that do not meet the requirements of any of the current products, and if you are able to, you should use these versions of Docker instead. If you are using the current Docker Desktop applications for Mac or for Windows, you can choose Kitematic from the menus within those applications, which will then start the installation process of Kitematic. You also have the option of downloading Kitematic directly from the Kitematic releases page.

Once you have installed Kitematic, you can start the application. On Desktop systems, this means clicking on the app icon. You will then be asked to log in with your Docker ID and user name. You also have the option to skip this step for now, and to browse Docker Hub as a guest, however. Once you have entered the application, you can then run applications through it. You can also find a list of all running and stopped containers on the left side of the application interface, underneath the link called "New Container." This list includes all of the containers, including ones that were not started through Kitematic, which can give you a quick and easy way to view and manage your containers. From there, you can view the logs from any container by clicking on that container. You can also restart or stop that container as well.

Docker Hub also has a page called "New Container," which allows you to search for new container images within the docker Hub to select. When you have found the specific image that you are looking for, you can run it by clicking the "create" option in order to pull that from the hub and run it.

If you select a container that is paused or stopped you can also restart or stop that container. Additionally, you will be able to view the container's output logs, and you can make any changes that you wish to make in the settings section, which will then be applied to the container if you restart it. You can also view all of the container's log outputs by clicking on the "Logs" preview or the "logs" tab. Once you have opened the logs, you can scroll through them and edit the logs as you wish. Any changes made will be applied upon restart.

Chapter 5

Public Repositories

This chapter is about Docker Hub. This topic has been talked about briefly in previous chapters, as well, but will be discussed in more detail in this chapter as well. Docker hub is the largest repository around the world of unique container images from a wide variety of sources, including various developers within the community and independent vendors for containers. Docker Hub users can gain access to all of the public repositories within the community for free and can choose a paid subscription to gain access to private repositories as well. Docker Hub's repositories are meant to allow you to share your own container images with customers, team members, or the docker community as a whole.

You can move container images to the Hub with the "Docker Push" command, and place them in a repository that way. Additionally, multiple images are able to be stored within a single repository as well. Multiple images can be added to a repository if you simply add a tag that is specific to that repository. Once you have done this, you will also be able to use the "Docker Push" command to push that repository to the appropriate registry for its name or tags. In order to "push" a repository If you want to create your own repositories, you first need to sign in to Docker Hub. Once you have signed if, you can click on the "Repositories" option, and then click on "Create Repo." When you are making a new repository, you have the option of putting it in your own Docker ID namespace or any other namespace that you are an "owner" of. When creating a repository, it is also important to note that the name of a repository does have to be unique within its namespace. Repository names can contain a minimum of 2 characters and a maximum of 255, and they can contain only lowercase letters, numbers hyphens, and underscores. The "short description" of a repository is what will be used for the purpose of search results, and will contain the first 100 characters of the "full description," which will function as the repository's "ReadMe." Once you have created a repository and titled it, you will be able to place container images into the repository with the "Docker Push" command. The images you've moved to the Hub will then be uploaded and made available to the community.

If you have access to private repositories, however, you will also be able to make your container images private, restricting them to people who have been granted access, which can either be your own account only or any account within a specific group. In order to create a private repository, you can simply select the "private" option when you are creating the repository. You can also change the settings of a repository that has already been created in order to make it private by going into its settings tab. You gain access to one private repository with your Docker Hub free account, as well, however, this free private repository will not be available to anyone but yourself. If you want to create more private repositories to share with other people you can upgrade your account with a paid Docker Hub subscription plan from the "Billing Information" page.

Once your private repository has been created, you will then be able to move your container image files to and from the repository. It is important to note that you will need to be signed in to an account that has access to a private repository in order to work with it. Additionally, private repositories can not currently be searched for through Docker's search tools. However, you are able to allow certain people or groups of people access to these private repositories, and manage their access to that repository from its settings page. You will also be able to change a repository's status between public and private if you so choose, at any time, provided you have an available slot open at that time.

A collaborator, in this context, refers to another individual who you can share access to your own private repositories with. Once you have designated a collaborator and given them access to your private repositories, they will then be able to push and pull to and from those private repositories. However, they will not be able to delete the repository or change its status from private to public, nor will they be able to perform any other sort of administrative task within those repositories, such as adding additional collaborators or restricting access from existing ones. You will also, as the owner, have the ability to change the level of the permissions to your collaborators on Docker

Hub by using organizations and teams to separate certain groups of people into categories and distinct groups.

You can also view the Docker Hub's repository "Tage" in order to see all of the tags that are available as well as the size of the image that is associated with each tag. The size of an image is an expression of all of the space that is taken up by a particular image as well as each of that image's "parent" images. The image size is also a representation of the disk space that all of the contents of the image's .tar file will take up when you save that image. In order to edit the tags of a particular repository, you simply need to click on the "Manage Repository" option or find that specific repository under "Repositories." You can search within the Docker Hub's registry with the search bar included in the Hub's interface, or by using the command line to search. When you search the Docker Hub registry in either of these ways, you will be able to locate specific images based on the name of the image, the name of the user who created the image, or the description of the image. Once you have located the image that you are searching for, you are able to then download that image with the command "docker pull <image name>:." You can also use the "star" feature of Docker Hub to mark specific images to return to at a later time. Your own images can be starred by other people, as well. The "star" feature is simply a quick and easy way to "bookmark" images that you particularly like or that you would like to revisit at a later time.

Chapter 6

Private Registries

The previous chapter of this book went over the topic of public repositories. While somewhat similar to that concept, this chapter's topic, which will be referred to as the "private registry." Docker Registry is another of the incredibly useful products that Docker provides to its users. This enterprise-grade solution is meant for the storage of various docker container images. In simple terms, Docker Registry is a service that can help you to easily and efficiently store your Container images and can be incredibly helpful for storing these images especially if you might not want your container images to be available to anyone else within the community, like with repositories stored on the Docker Hub. Private registries can be incredibly useful if you want to be able to easily manage the place where you store all of your container images. Docker Registry is also completely open-source, as well, in case you might want to alter it or add on to the application in any way.

The Docker Registry is compatible with version 1.6.0 or newer versions of the Docker engine, but Docker recommends that users who want a simpler solution that is "ready to go" and doesn't require any maintenance should instead try the Docker Hub, which can supply its users with a free hosted registry with many useful features and the option for more useful features that come with a paid subscription. The strengths and uses of the Docker Hub were discussed in the previous chapter in more depth, as well.

The Docker registry's storage is confined to drivers. The storage driver that the registry uses by default is in the local POSIX file system, in order to best suit development. However, many other cloud-based storage drivers can also be used. Developers who intend to use other storage locations can even write their own drivers. Additionally, the Docker Registry puts a very strong focus on your ability to secure access to your container images and also supports basic authentication and TLS as well. More information regarding advanced authorization and authentication methods can be found within the Docker Registry's GitHub repository.

The next topic that will be important to understand with regards to the Docker Registry is image naming. The names of various container images are used in many different docker commands. For example, the command "Docker pull ubuntu" will tell docker to "pull," or retrieve an image called "ubuntu" from the Docker Hub. This can serve as an incredibly handy shortcut for another much more lengthy command, "pull docker.io/library/ubuntu." Another very useful example of this is the "docker pull myregistrydomain:port/foo/bar" command. This can tell docker to find a registry within the location " myregistrydomain:port" in order to find and pull a specific image called "foo/bar." These are just a couple of the many different docker commands that deal directly with various images. You can also find more and learn more about many more of the different docker commands of this type in the Docker Engine's official documentation page.

Being able to run your own private registries is very easy and can complement your own continuous integration or continuous delivery systems, as well. In a normal type of workflow, any changes that are made to the source revision control system would also automatically prompt a build to be made on to your CI system as well, which would then push the new image to your docker registry, provided the build was not interrupted or prevented in some way. Once this has been completed, the registry would then be notified and would then prompt a deployment to be made for other systems also to be notified that a new container image has been made available in the registry. This is very useful for situations when you may want to deploy a new container image to a number of different machines. This is also the most effective and efficient method available to help you easily distribute a specific container image within an isolated network.

In order to use these private registries, it is recommended that you already have a familiarity with Docker. Specifically, you should be familiar with the processes of pushing and pulling docker container images. You will need to recognize the various differences between the cli and daemon as well and have a functional understanding of the basics of networking as well. While simply creating a docker private registry can be fairly easy to accomplish, being able to operate it as well will require a few additional skills, as is usually the case with most things. It is also strongly recommended that you have a familiarity with the concepts and basics of logging, log processing, systems availability and scalability, systems monitoring, and security technologies and a decent grasp of HTTP and general network communications, as well. Having a good handle on these and other similar skills can make it much easier for you to learn and understand, and even master, the various different features of Docker's private registries and how to use them.

Chapter 7

Linking Containers

This chapter will go over the concept and process of linking containers. It will also contain information about various topics related to the linking of containers, as well, such as the process of connecting with a network port and how to actually link containers. It will be very important for you to note during this chapter, however, that the link flag is considered to be a legacy feature of Docker. For Docker's users, this essentially means that the link flag feature may eventually be removed in the future. Unless for whatever reason, you have no other option than to continue to use this feature, it is strongly advised that you instead choose to use user-defined networks to help you to communicate between multiple different containers as opposed to using the link feature. It is recognized that there are features that the link feature is able to do that user-defined networks may not be able to, such as the sharing of environment variables between containers. While user defines networks do not possess this capability, there are several workarounds and other mechanisms that can be used in its place, such as using volumes to share various types of information between multiple containers. Before the Docker networks feature was released, Docker Links could be used to allow easy and effective communication and secure data transfers between different containers. With the addition of the Docker Networks feature to Docker's impressive list of products and services, users are still able to create links between containers, but they function in slightly different ways between the default bridge network and user-defined ones.

As has been mentioned in earlier chapters of this book, each container that you create needs to have a name in order to finalize its creation, and will automatically assign a name to each container by default. You can also rename a container to something else if you want to do so. This can be done if you use the "name" flag, and you will also have the option to return the container's name with docker inspect. It is important to remember that each container's name must be unique. This means that two containers can not share the same name. This can be important to remember when assigning new names to your containers. If you want to use a name for a container that is already assigned to another one, you have first to delete the original container or assign it a new name before you can assign that name to the new container.

Docker uses the names of these containers for all tasks related to the sorting and organization of your containers. This included the establishment of links between these different containers. These names can help to organize your containers for both docker and yourself. Of course, the names of different containers can be useful to you to help you to remember which containers are which and the purposes that they serve. Additionally, Docker can also use the names of all of your different containers to identify and organize all of your containers, and it uses these names as reference points when creating links as well.

Links between containers can enable these containers to easily find each other in order to transfer data from one container to the other. By creating these links between different containers, you create a path for information to travel on from the first container, which serves as the source, to the second, which is called the recipient. This is a one-way path that allows the recipient to gain access to specific information from the source container. In order to actually create a link from one container to another, you simply need to use the "link" flag.

The first step that you will need to take in order to do this is to create a new container that contains a database. This can be done by creating your new container from the training/Postgres container image, which will then contain within it a PostgreSQL database. Once this step has been completed, you can create a new container to link to the first one with the database. "$ docker run -d -P --name [new container name] --link [name of database container]:[alias]/webapp python app.py" will allow you to link this new container to the first container with the database. The bracketed spaces should, of course, be replaced with the appropriate names where the new container is the recipient container, and the database container name and alias will represent the name and alias of the original "source" container. Once this has been completed, and your two containers have been successfully linked, you can inspect these two containers with Docker Inspect. When you do this, you should be able to see that the two containers are now linked, with the recipient container being able to retrieve information from the source. The recipient container will now be able to access various information about and from the source container and its database.

Chapter 8

Docker Commands

The next important thing that you will want to understand when you are learning about Docker and all of its various features are the commands. This chapter will be discussing the docker commands and how actually to use them effectively. This will be a very important aspect of mastering docker and getting use out of it. Depending on how your docker system is configured, it is possible that you might have to preface each of your docker commands with sudo. If you are not familiar with sudo, it stands for "substitute user do" or "super user do." Sudo can be incredibly helpful and even critical to some Linux distributions and can be useful when you are attempting to run administrative applications. In simple terms, sudo can allow one user to run a program as another user, which is most often the root user. If you want to avoid the need to use sudo with the docker command, then you (or the system administrator) will need to create a "docker" unix group and then add users to that group. Otherwise, you will need to rely on "sudo" with your docker commands.

The next things that will need to be discussed in this chapter are the configuration files. The Docker command line will typically store all of its configuration files within a directory that is named .docker, that exists within your home directory by default. You are able, however, to change this and specify a new location for these files to go to with the "DOCKER_CONFIG" environment variable. You also have the option to use the "-config" command-line option, but it will be important to note that if you use both of these methods, then the "-config" option will take priority over "DOCKER_CONFIG" and will override any settings made by using that method. Additionally, Docker uses the configuration directory and will automatically store and manage the files in this directory itself. As such, it is strongly advised that you do not modify any of these files. You can, however, safely change or modify the file called "config.json" in order to change or alter the specific ways in which the docker command will act. Docker users have the ability to change or alter the docker command behavior by using various command-line options and environment variables. Users are also able to alter various options in the config.json file to change many of the same behaviors. When you are changing and modifying these behaviors, it can be very important to consider the order of priority among these various mechanisms. For example, any command-line options that are used will automatically take priority over any environment variables that are used, and these environment variables will be prioritized over any properties that are specified in a "config.json" file. There are a number of various properties that are stored within the config.json file, which will be listed below:

HttpHeaders: The "HttpHeaders" property specifies a collection of different headers that will be included within any an all of the messages that may be sent from the Docker client to the daemon. The daemon will be discussed in the chapter on the Docker engine. In simple terms, the daemon is able to accept docker API requests and communicate with other daemons in order to manage a number of different services. Docker is not able to interpret any of these headers, and it also cannot allow these headers to affect any headers that it sets for itself. They are simply put into all of the messages that they are applied to without any effect on any other headers that docker has set for itself.

psFormat: The "psFormat" property will specify the format that is used by default for the docker ps output. If the docker ps command is used and the "--format" flag is not provided, the Docker client will automatically refer to the psFormat property for this purpose. If the psFormat property has not been set, then the docker client will then refer to the default table format, instead.

imagesFormat: The "imagesFormat" property will specify the format that is used by default for the purpose of docker images output. If the docker images command is used and the "--format" flag is not provided with it, the docker client will automatically refer to the imagesFormat property for this purpose. If the imagesFormat property has not been set, then the docker client will then refer instead to the default table format for this purpose.

pluginsFormat: The "pluginsFormat" property will specify the format that is used by default for the purpose of docker plugin ls output. If the docker plugin ls command is used and the "--format" flag is not provided with it, the docker client will automatically refer to the pluginsFormat property for this purpose. If the pluginsFormat property has not been set, then the docker client will then refer instead to the default table format for this purpose.

servicesFormat: The "servicesFormat" property will specify the format that is used by default for the purpose of docker service ls output. If the docker service ls command is used and the "--format" flag is not provided with it, the docker client will automatically refer to the serviceFormat property for this purpose. If the servicesFormat property has not been set, then the docker client will then refer instead to the default table format for this purpose.

serviceInspectFormat: The "serviceInspectFormat" property will specify the format that is used by default for the purpose of docker service inspect the output. If the docker service inspects command is used, and the "--format" flag is not provided with it, the docker client will automatically refer to the serviceInspectFormat property for this purpose. If the servicesFormat property has not been set, then the docker client will then refer instead to the default json format for this purpose.

statsFormat: The "servicesFormat" property will specify the format that is used by default for the purpose of docker stats ls output. If the docker stats command is used and the "--format" flag is not provided with it, the docker client will automatically refer to the statsFormat property for this purpose. If the statsFormat property has not been set, then the docker client will then refer instead to the default table format for this purpose.

secretFormat: The "secretFormat" property will specify the format that is used by default for the purpose of docker secret ls output. If the docker secret ls command is used and the "--format" flag is not provided with it, the docker client will automatically refer to the secretFormat property for this purpose. If the secretFormat property has not been set, then the docker client will then refer instead to the default table format for this purpose.

nodesFormat: The "nodesFormat" property will specify the format that is used by default for the purpose of docker node ls output. If the docker node ls command is used and the "--format" flag is not provided with it, the docker client will automatically refer to the nodesFormat property and will use the value of the nodesFormat for this purpose. If the nodesFormat property has not been set with a value, then the docker client will then refer instead to the default table format for this purpose.

configFormat: The "configFormat" property will specify the format that is used by default for the purpose of docker config ls output. If the docker config ls command is used and the "--format" flag is not provided with it, the docker client will automatically refer to the configFormat property for this purpose. If the configFormat property has not been set, then the docker client will then refer instead to the default table format for this purpose.

credsStore: the "credsStore" property will specify an external binary that will be used as the credential store by default. When the credsStore property has been set, docker login will automatically try to use the external binary that has been specified by "docker-credential-<value>" for the purpose of storing credentials. This binary can be easily viewed within $PATH. If the credsStore property has not been set, then the docker client will then default to using the auths property of the config for the purpose of storing these credentials.

credHelpers: The "credHelpers" property will specify a group of credential helpers that will be used by default for the purposes of storing or retrieving credentials for specific registries. These credential helpers will automatically take priority over the credsStore property or auths for the purposes of the storage and retrieval of any relevant credentials. If the credHelpers property has not been set, then the docker client will then refer instead to the docker-credential-<value> binary by default for the purposes of the storage or retrieval of any relevant credentials for specific registries.

stackOrchestrator. The "stackOrhestrator" property will specify the orchestrator that is used by default for the purpose of running any docker stack management commands. Values that will be considered valid for this purpose include "all," "kubernetes," "swarm." It is also possible to override this property by using the "--orchestrator" flag, or by using the "DOCKER_STACK_ORCHESTRATOR" environment variable.

More information about all of these properties and various other useful features can be found within the relevant sections of the docker login documentation, as well.

Chapter 9

Docker Engine

The next topic that will be important to discuss when you are attempting to master docker is the Docker Engine. This was discussed briefly in an earlier chapter of this book but will be covered in more detail here, as well. The Docker engine can be described as a platform meant to help developers to create, run, and ship various applications. When people say "Docker," they are usually either referring to the company called Docker, or the product created by the Docker company, called the Docker Engine. The Docker engine allows its users to create and run applications, which are largely separate from their system's infrastructure by using containers. These containers can allow applications to run consistently, regardless of the system that they are being run on. By using the Docker Engine's unique methods of testing, shipping, and deploying your applications, you can significantly reduce the time that it takes to create container-based applications that run efficiently regardless of the system.

Docker can give its users the ability to pack up an application into a largely isolated (or contained) environment, which is referred to as a container, and then run that application from the container. This isolation can provide extra security as well as making it easier for you to run multiple different containers at the same time on a particular system. Containers can be very "lightweight" because of their ability to be run directly within the kernel of the machine that they are being hosted on, which eliminates the need for a hypervisor. This is a very helpful feature and is what allows for multiple different containers to be run on a single system much more efficiently than if the applications were being run from their own separate virtual machines. You can imagine how much more taxing this can be on a single machine as opposed to simply being able to run each application on its own. Docker containers are even able to be run inside virtual machines acting as their hosts if a user required this capability.

Docker can help to speed up the development lifecycle and make the development of these applications even more efficient by enabling developers to create applications within standardized environments by using local containers for various applications and services. This can make containers especially helpful to workflows that rely on continuous integration or continuous delivery, as well.

The Docker Engine can also allow for much more portable workloads than any other product or service on the market with its container-based platform. With these containers, Docker's users can run applications on a wide variety of different environments, such as a developer's personal computer, a virtual machine in a data center, or even on a cloud provider. Docker's unique container-based platform and its portable nature make it much easier to manage all of your applications effectively and efficiently.

The Docker Engine's architecture relies on a client-server relationship. The Docker client will communicate with the docker "daemon," which is what actually does most of the work involving your docker containers. The docker daemon does not have to run on the same system, although it can definitely do that as well. The docker client is capable of connecting to a remote docker daemon, meaning that they can also be run on different systems if you choose to run them this way. This is because the Docker daemon will communicate with your client by using a REST API over a network interface. The Docker darmon is able to "listen" for requests from the Docker API and manage various objects such as containers, images, networks, and volumes within Docker as well. The Docker Daemon can even communicate with other darmons just as it communicates with your client in order to more effectively manage various services provided by Docker. Of course, the primary way that the docker daemon will be useful to you is through the docker client. The client is the main way that you will be able to make use of the daemon. When you use a command within the docker client, it will then send that command to the daemon, which will then process and complete those commands. It can also be helpful to note that a single Docker client is able to communicate with multiple daemons, in the same way, that the daemon can communicate with other daemons as well.

Another very useful feature of the Docker Engine is the registry. Docker registries are spaces that are used to store various docker container images. The Docker Hub and Docker Cloud are good examples of public registries. These services can be used by anyone.

Docker is even specifically programmed to default to the Docker Hub when it searches for specific container images. While there are public registries that you can gain access to and use if you wish, you can also choose to create and run your own private ones, as well. If you use the "docker pull" or the "docker run" command, the images that you need will then be retrieved from the registry that you have configured. The "docker push" command will, of course, push an image to the registry that you have configured.

Chapter 10

Docker Swarm

The next topic that will need to be understood in order to gain a complete mastery of Docker and its products is the swarm. Most of Docker's other features function with a single host, being your own local machine, but docker can also be switched into a "swarm mode." A "swarm" can be described as a collection of machines that are all running docker simultaneously. Once these machines have all been clustered together, you can continue to run docker commands as normal, but they will need to be executed within the cluster by the swarm manager. The swarm manager is the only machine within a specific cluster that is able to execute commands made within the cluster, and is also exclusively able to bring additional machines into the cluster as "workers." When you activate the swarm mode on a specific machine, that machine will automatically become the manager of its swarm, with a collection of additional worker machines. A worker machine, of course, can not execute any commands or tell other machines what they can and can not do. The worker machine exists inside the cluster exclusively to provide a little bit of extra capacity.

These "worker" machines are typically referred to as "nodes," or "Docker nodes." While it is possible to run a single node or even multiple nodes from a single physical machine or from a cloud server, most docker swarm deployments are typically made up of several docker nodes that have been divided across multiple machines of these kinds. If a worker node wants to deploy a specific application within a swarm that it is a part of, they will need to submit a service definition to the swarm's manager. The manager will then need to send small units of work to be done (these are referred to as "tasks") to the worker nodes within the swarm. Once these tasks have been distributed to the worker nodes, and they have been received, the worker nodes can begin to execute the tasks that they have been assigned. This will include the manager nodes as well, as they are also set by default to function as worker nodes as well as swarm managers. However, it is possible to configure their settings and have them function exclusively as manager nodes. The tasks assigned to each node are monitored by an assigned agent, and the current states of each of the swarm's worker nodes will be reported to the manager in order to help the swarm manager to maintain an ideal state within the swarm.

One of the most significant advantages of using the swarm mode with docker instead of a single machine is the ability to alter or change the configuration of a specific service without having to restart that service manually. Docker will simply update this configuration automatically. Once the configuration has been updated, all of the service's current tasks that use the original one will be stopped, and then recreated with the new and updated configuration. Additionally, the swarm manager can set an "optimal state" for their swarm at the time of the swarm's creation, and docker will then manage the swarm in order to maintain that state as consistently as possible within the swarm. If one of the swarm's worker nodes becomes unavailable for some reason, then Docker will automatically redistribute all of the tasks that were assigned to that worker node to other worker nodes within the swarm. You can also run additional standalone docker containers along with any swarm services that are being run while running in swarm mode. Any Docker daemon is capable of serving in a swarm as a manager or a worker, or both simultaneously, and while swarm services can only be managed by the swarm's manager, standalone docker containers are able to be run from any daemon.

The Docker Swarm is centered primarily around the tasks that are divided up amongst and carried out by the manager and worker nodes within the swarm. These tasks are most often referred to as "services," and they function as the main basis of any interaction that occurs between the user and the Docker swarm itself. When a service is created, it will ask for you to specify the container image that you would like to use, as well as the specific commands that will be executed within any containers that are being run by the service. There are different ays that tasks can be divided up among the nodes within a particular swarm, as well. For example, wif a "replicated services" model is used, then the swarm's manager will distribute a particular number of "replica tasks" to all of the worker nodes that exist within the swarm. This number is based on the scale that was set for the swarm's desired state. In the case of a global service model, the swarm will distribute tasks for the service that is being run evenly among each node within the cluster that is available at the time of distribution.

Each available node will receive one task with this kind of service model. Each task that is assigned to a worker node will carry with it its own docker container, and all of the specific commands that it will need to run inside that container, as well. The manager node will assign these tasks to the worker nodes based on the number of replicas that have been set within the service scale. Additionally, a task can not be transferred to another node once it has been assigned. The task can only be run on the node that it was assigned to. Otherwise, it will fail.

Additionally, it can be important to note for these purposes that you do have the option to use the Docker Desktop application for Mac or for Windows in order to test the features of swarm mode that deal with single nodes. This includes the initialization of a single node swarm, as well as the creation and scaling of various services. Docker "Moby" and "Hyper-V" will function as the single node swarms for Mac and Windows operating systems, respectively. However, it is currently not possible for the Docker Desktop application to test a swarm with multiple nodes on its own. This applies to both the Mac and Windows versions of Docker Desktop, as well.

You are allowed to use the Docker Machine that has been included with these applications in order to create the swarm nodes that you will need. You can run your commands from the Docker Desktop application on a Mac or Windows host, but that host itself is not able to participate in the swarm that is created. Once the swarm's nodes have been created, you will be able to run all of the swarm commands as they are shown in the Mac Terminal or Windows PowerShell, as long as the Docker Desktop application stays running.

Conclusion

Congratulations! At this point, you should have a much better idea of Docker and all of its various products and services, as well as how to use those products and services to help you to maximize your efficiency in building and running container-based applications.

This step by step guide to learning and mastering Docker has been designed to help you do exactly what it says on the cover; learn and master Docker. This incredibly helpful book is meant to serve as your guide in understanding many of the various different products and services that Docker offers to its users, as well as a number of the different features that exist within those products and services and how to use them as effectively as possible in order to maximize the benefits of using this incredibly unique service. Additionally, this book has gone over all of the little ins and outs of the Docker platform and its various products and services, including some tips, tricks, and shortcuts to help you even further in this goal.

This book went over a number of different topics to give you all of the tools necessary to gain a complete understanding and mastery over Docker's various products and services. These topics included things like the various reasons why you would (and should) choose Docker over any other possibly similar service as well as some short introductions and guides to many of the various products and services that docker offers to its users such as Docker Enterprise and Docker

Desktop for Mac or Windows, and the Docker Hub. This book also went over many of the different features of Docker's various products and services, as well as how to actually use them at a fundamental level in order to help you to master this incredibly innovative platform for building and running applications as smoothly and efficiently as possible.

With all of that said and out of the way, I would like to offer one last word of gratitude to you for taking the initiative and purchasing this book, and another short congratulation for taking the steps necessary to understand and master the Docker platform and its various services. At this point, you should have all of the tools necessary to help you to learn how to use Docker's products and services as effectively as possible and to get the most out of these very innovative tools.